Wild Rides!

Roller Coasters

By A. R. Schaefer

Consultant:
Steve M. Wren
Iowa Representative
American Coaster Enthusiasts

Capstone press

Mankato, Minnesota

Edge Books are published by Capstone Press
151 Good Counsel Drive, P.O. Box 669, Mankato, Minnesota 56002
www.capstonepress.com

Library of Congress Cataloging-in-Publication Data
Schaefer, A. R. (Adam Richard), 1976–
    Roller coasters / by A. R. Schaefer.
    p. cm.—(Edge Books, Wild rides!)
    Includes bibliographical references and index.
    ISBN 0-7368-2726-9 (hardcover)
    1. Roller coasters—Juvenile literature. 2. Roller coasters—History—Juvenile
literature. [1. Roller coasters.] I. Title. II. Series.
GV1860.R64S34 2005
688.7—dc22   2003027107

Summary: Discusses roller coasters, including their history, design, and
    popularity today.

Editorial Credits
Donald Lemke, editor; Kia Adams, series designer; Patrick D. Dentinger,
    book designer; Jo Miller, photo researcher; Eric Kudalis, product
    planning editor

Photo Credits
Corbis/AFP, 17; Bettmann, 10; Jay Dickman, 21; Lake County Museum, 13;
    Michele Westmorland, 18–19; Stapleton Collection, 8
Folio Inc./Jeffery MacMillan, cover, 24–25
Getty Images Inc./Mario Tama, 28
Index Stock Imagery/James Lemass, 14; Mark Gibson, 4; Timothy O'Keefe, 22
Mira/Skip Gandy, 7
The Image Finders/Jim Baron, 20, 27
Unicorn Stock Photos/Julie Walker, 16

1 2 3 4 5 6 09 08 07 06 05 04

Table of Contents

Chapter One: Roller Coasters 5

Chapter Two: Early Roller
Coasters....................9

Chapter Three: Designing a
Roller Coaster 15

Chapter Four: Famous Roller
Coasters 23

Glossary 30

Read More 31

Internet Sites.................................... 31

Index 32

Learn about:

- **Roller coaster cars**

- **Out-and-back coasters**

- **Twister coasters**

CHAPTER **1**

Roller Coasters

The roller coaster creeps to the top of the first hill. Thirty riders grab their lap bars. Suddenly, they are traveling toward the ground at 60 miles (95 kilometers) per hour. Everyone screams. Some people raise their arms up in the air.

The riders gasp as the coaster takes a hard right turn. Just as quickly, the coaster climbs another hill and picks up speed as it races down. Then the cars go upside down in a loop. The riders can see people walking on the ground. A few seconds later, the coaster is back at the station. Thirty more people are ready to ride.

Types of Roller Coasters

The first coasters in the United States were small and made of wood. Today, roller coasters come in all shapes and sizes. But every roller coaster has a car and a track.

Roller coaster cars can be above the track or below the track. They can be stand-up or sit-down cars. Some coasters have several cars that are hooked together. Other coasters have only one car.

Roller coaster tracks have many designs. One of the oldest coaster designs is called an out-and-back. These coasters travel in a straight line over several hills. The cars make a big turn and head back to the starting point. Twister coasters have quick turns and drops. They can fit on a small area of land. Corksrew coasters have spirals that turn riders upside down.

The Python at Busch Gardens in Tampa, Florida, is a corkscrew roller coaster.

Learn about:

- **Russian ice slides**

- **The Pennsylvania railway ride**

- **Gravity Pleasure Switchback Railway**

CHAPTER 2

Early Roller Coasters

The idea behind the roller coaster started in Russia about 400 years ago. During winter, people poured water onto a wooden slide. When the water froze, people carried sleds to the top of the slide. They would then ride the sleds down the ice.

First Roller Coasters

A French traveler in Russia saw the giant ice slides. He thought people in France would like these rides. But the weather in France was not cold enough for an ice slide. In the early 1800s, the French built cars with wheels, or rollers. The cars locked into a grooved track and coasted down a hill. Many people believe this is how the term roller coaster started.

Soon, the French developed the first circuit ride. A circuit ride begins and ends in the same place. This design was easier than carrying sleds to the top of a hill.

During the early 1800s, people enjoyed coasters at amusement parks in Paris, France.

Mauch Chunk Switchback Railway

The first roller coaster in the United States started as a railway. During the mid-1800s, a Pennsylvania mining company used railway cars to move coal. Mules pulled the cars up tracks to the top of a mine hill. The cars were loaded with coal and sent back down. They coasted to the bottom of the hill.

In 1873, the railway started carrying people instead of coal. The Mauch Chunk Switchback Railway became a popular ride. Thousands of people paid to coast down the hill in a railway car.

Early U.S. Coasters

The Gravity Pleasure Switchback Railway was the first U.S. coaster designed as a ride. It opened on Coney Island, New York, in 1884. The coaster could reach a top speed of 6 miles (10 kilometers) per hour.

Switchback coasters had two towers. A single car started at the top of the first tower. The car traveled down a series of hills to the bottom of the second tower. Workers in the second tower raised the car to the top. They put the car on another track and sent it back to the first tower.

Soon, U.S. coaster makers designed circuit tracks. Most early circuit coasters were called scenic railways. These coasters traveled through lighted tunnels. The tunnels were often painted with mountains or other outdoor scenes.

Ups and Downs

In the early 1900s, amusement park owners built more roller coasters. Many of these coasters had big hills and turns. Some of them turned riders upside down. By the 1920s, there were almost 2,000 coasters in North America.

During the Great Depression (1929–1939),
most people didn't have enough money to enjoy
coasters. Many of the rides were torn down. By
the 1960s, only about 200 coasters remained
in the United States.

Learn about:

- **Lift hills**

- **Brakes**

- **Guide wheels**

CHAPTER **3**

Designing a Roller Coaster

Modern roller coasters are difficult to build and design. In the early days, all people needed was a track, a sled, and a hill. Today, design teams, physicists, and testers all work together. They use computers and other equipment to make the rides safe and fun.

Track Design

Designing a new roller coaster is not easy. A poorly designed coaster might stop in the middle of the track or fail to stop at the station. The coaster could also make riders uncomfortable or sick.

A chain lift pulls roller coaster cars up the first hill.

Most roller coaster tracks start with a lift hill. A rolling chain under the track pulls coaster cars up this hill. The cars have chain dogs on the sides or bottom. These hooks attach to the chain. As the chain moves up the hill, it pulls the cars along.

The lift hill is the tallest hill on the track. The chain dogs release the coaster cars at the top of the lift hill. The force of gravity pulls the cars down. The cars gain speed as they travel down the first hill. Most roller coasters reach speeds of 50 to 60 miles (80 to 95 kilometers) per hour. Some new roller coasters can travel more than 100 miles (160 kilometers) per hour.

The first hill of the Steel Dragon 2000 in Nagashima, Japan, drops 306 feet (93 meters).

Speed from the first hill propels the cars through the rest of the ride. Some rides have small hills and sharp turns. Other roller coasters have giant loops. These rides are called looping coasters.

Coaster Brakes

Some tracks have brakes in the middle. Brakes keep the coaster cars from going too fast around corners. They also stop the coaster at the end of the ride.

The Mine Trains at Ocean Park in Hong Kong has sharp turns and small hills.

Coaster Car Wheels

Most coaster cars have three kinds of wheels. Road wheels sit on top of the track. Upstop wheels sit under the track. These wheels keep coaster cars from flying off at the top of a hill. The third wheel is called a guide wheel. This wheel goes sideways against the track. It keeps the cars from sliding off during a turn.

Wheels keep roller coaster cars connected to the track.

Safety Gear

Roller coaster cars are designed to be safe and comfortable for riders. Today, most roller coasters have two pieces of safety gear. The first is a seat belt. The other is a large restraint. On some coasters, this restraint comes over the rider's head. Other coasters have restraints that lock in the rider at the waist.

Learn about:

- **The green machine**

- **The world's tallest and fastest**

- **National Historic Landmark**

CHAPTER **4**

Famous Roller Coasters

Roller coasters are favorite rides at many amusement parks. In 2004, there were more than 1,800 roller coasters around the world. The Incredible Hulk and the Top Thrill Dragster were two of the most popular.

The Incredible Hulk

Today, many roller coasters are based on movies, TV shows, or comic books. The Incredible Hulk Coaster opened in 1999. It is part of Universal's Islands of Adventure in Orlando, Florida.

Many riders are surprised by the power of the Incredible Hulk Coaster. This green machine starts by moving forward slowly. Suddenly, the cars rocket uphill at 40 miles (65 kilometers) per hour.

Soon, the ride reaches almost 70 miles (110 kilometers) per hour. It turns upside down seven times before returning to the station. The entire ride lasts two minutes and 15 seconds.

The Incredible Hulk Coaster turns riders upside down seven times.

Top Thrill Dragster

In 2003, the Top Thrill Dragster opened at Cedar Point in Sandusky, Ohio. This amusement park is known for building huge rides. The $25 million Dragster is the world's tallest coaster. It is also the fastest.

The Dragster starts with a hydraulic launch system. This system shoots the coaster cars out of the station. In only four seconds, the cars are going 120 miles (193 kilometers) per hour. At full speed, the cars climb 420 feet (128 meters) into the air. The cars turn at the top of the hill and twist back down. Within 22 seconds, this record-breaking ride is over.

In 2003, the Top Thrill Dragster became the tallest and fastest coaster in the world.

The Cyclone

During the 1920s, the United States experienced a roller coaster boom. Amusement parks built many coasters. On June 26, 1927, the Cyclone opened on Coney Island in New York.

At more than 85 feet (26 meters) tall, the Cyclone was an instant success. People from around the country wanted to experience the huge first drop. They had heard about the Cyclone's eight giant hills. Within one year, ticket sales had paid for the cost of building the ride.

In the early 1970s, the Cyclone was almost torn down. Many people were upset. Eventually, a company bought the coaster and fixed it up. The Cyclone reopened in 1975. In 1991, the coaster became a National Historic Landmark. Today, people can still ride the famous Cyclone.

Glossary

amusement park (uh-MYOOZ-muhnt PARK)—a place where people pay to go on rides, play games, and enjoy other kinds of entertainment

circuit (SUR-kit)—a circular route; a circuit track begins and ends in the same place.

gravity (GRAV-uh-tee)—the force that pulls things down toward the surface of the earth

hydraulic (hye-DRAW-lik)—a machine that creates power by forcing liquid under pressure through pipes

propel (pruh-PEL)—to drive or push something forward

restraint (ruh-STRAYNT)—something that holds something else back

scenic (SEE-nik)—having beautiful surroundings

Read More

Burgan, Michael. *The World's Wildest Roller Coasters.* Built for Speed. Mankato, Minn.: Capstone Press, 2001.

Greenberg, Daniel A. *Amusement Park Science.* Science Links. Philadelphia: Chelsea Clubhouse Books, 2003.

Stone, Lynn M. *Roller Coasters.* How Are They Built? Vero Beach, Fla.: Rourke, 2002.

Internet Sites

FactHound offers a safe, fun way to find Internet sites related to this book. All of the sites on FactHound have been researched by our staff.

Here's how:

1. Visit *www.facthound.com*

2. Type in this special code **0736827269** for age-appropriate sites. Or enter a search word related to this book for a more general search.

3. Click on the **Fetch It** button.

FactHound will fetch the best sites for you!

Index

amusement parks, 23, 26, 29
    Cedar Point, 26
    Universal's Islands of
        Adventure, 23

brakes, 19

car parts
    chain dogs, 16
    safety gear, 21
    wheels, 9, 20
Coney Island, 11, 29
Cyclone, 29

designs
    corksrew, 6
    looping, 18
    out-and-back, 6
    switchback, 11–12
    twister, 6

gravity, 16
Gravity Pleasure Switchback
    Railway, 11

Great Depression, 13

hydraulic launch system, 26

Incredible Hulk, 23–25

lift hill, 16

Mauch Chunk Switchback
    Railway, 11

railway, 11
riders, 5, 6, 11, 12, 15, 21, 24
Russian ice slides, 9

scenic railways, 12
speed, 5, 11, 16, 18, 24–25, 26
    world's fastest, 26
station, 5, 15, 25, 26

Top Thrill Dragster, 23, 26

world's tallest, 26